Inside The Kaleidoscope

By Derick D. Wright

We are people of royalty. People of color. The first to walk this planet. We are God's people. Well, that's what my father always told us. He's not only the leader of our household, but he's the leader of our tribe as well. He's a very strong willed and strong-minded person. True royalty and greatness. So many of our people depend on him for so many major decisions. I'm his first born. My name is Kyauta which in my culture means "Gift". My parents have in me and often said since birth that I'd be a gift for our people. Me myself, I don't know about all that. A simple life would satisfy me greatly. We have enough to do as is anyway. Hunting, fishing, farming, etc... my father says we have a solution to making work a little easier considering the conditions we face. The heat can be excruciating and sometimes fatal. Some areas are better some days. None the less, most of the land in which we farm, usually bears plenty fruit. Our people have this plan to go seek help from neighboring countries in order to solve our problems. We seem to think trade via condition is the solution. Basically, that means goods that are hunted and farmed in harsh conditions would be compromised vi trade. A benefit for benefit deal. So, if hunting for deer is too dangerous here but we have fruit, then we trade the fruit to those countries that have trouble growing them. In return for example, deer. Right off it sounds like a great idea, but the world is full of people ready to take advantage. With that being said, we'll see how that goes. According to sources, my father says, most countries have agreed to the deal. But it seems we have not come to an agreement with one entire continent, Europe. A continent rich in goods and ran by many great empires. Our governing body happens to see this as a real issue. Upon discussion, our people have come up with a decision to get Europe to cooperate. They called the mission, "Capture and Conquer". Basically, our military's job is to seize the continent

with war like tactics.
Instill fear in their
people to gain control.
In no time, our people
infiltrated their
borders and were
quickly met by their
military. Many of our
own were killed.
Amongst those was my
father. It was that day
I was made a man
and leader of my
tribe. The Capture
and Conquer mission

had begun to take shape. Before we knew it, we had the Europeans here in our lands. Disturbing as I may add, they were chained and caged like animals. A group of them were into our territory and I was given the tasks for them to complete each day. I'm officially an overseer of a group of people who aren't my own. I don't know their language, habits, tendencies, nothing. I was told that one or two of them knew our native language. I was told to label them by branding and giving them names that our people could understand clearly. Branding may seem a little harsh but, in our culture it's a way to describe who you are. Each tribe has a unique brand. My job was to brand them with my tribal mark. That way everyone knows who I'll be overseeing. Initially I noticed that this process wasn't taken kindly by the people. All the shouting and crying were universal sounds for pain and abuse. I ask myself; are we abusing them? I was soon asked to appoint some of my people to oversee the group due to the work I had as tribe leader. I sat in on a meeting that basically stated, "to preserve African life we must enslave those of white skin to perform the tasks that are in harsher conditions. I was told it was my father's vision to solve the problems of our land and preserving the lives of our people. BY ANY MEANS NECESSARY!! In this case, enslaving the Europeans. Our instructions were as follows:

Whites must hunt our land until no sun.

Whites must till dirt
until all land is
prepared for farming.

White must plant
seeds until fields are
filled.

If whites do not
cooperate, they must
be struck.

If no strikes are given,
we are then looked at
like traitors and are
punished by law.

If further discipline is needed for whites, it shall be fatal.

Such harsh rules in my opinion. It'll definitely take some getting used to. Time passes as the new comers are settling in. while checking the lands, I notice the real pain and suffering that their people are facing. The men belittled before their families like its nothing. The women beaten and separated from their children. I see tears roll down the face of a child as he begged for his mother. I see raw wounds from whips as they've destroyed their pale skin. The harsh conditions causing so many problems for their people. Most of them dying rapidly. I look upon them and see a broken people robbed of their native land and way of life. Suffering at the hands of their oppressor. In which was our people. I feel so guilty for being a part of madness. I want to help them but, as tribe leader I'm sure I'd be sentenced to die. I just try to imagine if it were our people being enslaved. Would I want us to be saved? What can I do to save them? I walked outside today and seen a family eliminated. Seeing people murdered the way I did today really pushed me to make a change. I began to address the conditions of the slaves and the ways they were being punished. I was quickly shut down. I was told that if I continue to talk this way I'd be viewed as a traitor to our people. I was also reminded that my father's vision was to see our people succeed in everyday task without the risk. Our statistics indicate that this has become a possibility due to his last mission. When put like that it sounds good but not at the expense of other's lives. I took it upon myself to build a campaign to free the enslaved Europeans. I began to earn their language more in depth. I was now able to communicate with them better. Seeing the scars, hearing about how the men were castrated, and how they were disposed of like trash really bothered me. I knew it was up to me to change this way of living. Word got out about my opinions on slavery. Rumors of me becoming a traitor were getting around quickly. I assure you, I'm no traitor. I simply want everyone to be treated equally. I mean at least let them go back home. During a court hearing I shouted, "free the slaves and let them go home!!" I was then apprehended and taken to solitary confinement. As I sit there, I ask God, "am

I wrong? Father is this how things were meant to be?" I was soon set free but relieved of my duties as leader. I was sentenced to one week of slavery in light conditions. This week felt as if it had tripled its duration. I had never seen work like this before. And these people were forced to do it daily.

It's sad to see to say the least. I haven't begun to scratch the surface as to what they're experiencing. I began explaining to them that death, to me, is far better than bondage. Also, God didn't create us to be slaves. He created us to be equal. We have an entire planet to share and we must understand our position beneath the stars. These words began to sink deep into the soon to be rebels of slavery. We then began creating an escape plan and route. Basically, I'd be forgiven after my week is done and will be appointed as an overseer. I plan to use that platform to lead the people to a distant land of freedom. This will be a hard task but it's worth the risk. The worst that may happen is death. Like I said though, death is better than bondage. If we die, we die with honor. I do believe we can make it though. I believe we'll set the blueprint for like minds to take their chance on freedom as well. The plan was now complete but will require a little time. I was now free of my sentence. I've been given the opportunity to be an overseer in order to gain back the trust of the people. With the reactions and attitudes of my people, I've gained some discomfort. So, for this plan to work I'd have to put on a façade, I must play the part to the best of my ability. I explained to the slaves that no matter what I will free them. I asked them to not take anything personal. It's all a part of the process. One thing I am opposed to is murder. I've established a tight bond with these people and taking their lives after what I witnessed them go through was out if the question. My name means Gift and I'm giving myself to them for their freedom. I'm willing to risk everything for a people that I do not belong to. I love my own, but they must see the evil in which has been casted upon the suffering. White or brown we are all the same. We all have families and a sole purpose on this planet. I know this because God has shown me my purpose. No one is put here to be treated like cattle, enslaved by man, and tortured by tyrants. To create a better way by bloodshed is never the way. Today I am sixteen. It's been five years since I lost my father. I have now begun the voyage to freedom for the enslaved Europeans. I've hidden boats, food, and other survival materials. In case of an emergency I hope they find it with no problem. I've left clues and notes to the entrusted incase I'm captured. On today I was invited to a festival. In order to keep the peace and relieve suspicion, I decided to attend. I arrived at the festival and the first thing I noticed was a decorated boat with the words "Voyage to Freedom" engraved on it. I was quickly approached and questioned. It was one of the boats I had set up for the escape. I see here of my entrusted men awaiting their hanging. I cried out in apologies to them.

As I was being detained, I was forced to watch these young white men hang. One yelled out, "Kyauta! Death is freedom from bondage! We all thank you! You were truly a gift." Kyauta was then stoned publicly by his own people and then dismantled. Destroyed by his own people because he saw fit that people of all color, race, and homeland should be equal. Also, those of greater power shouldn't take advantage of those of lesser power. His last words were, "I am free."

My name is
Alexander of
England. I am a
sixteen-year-old. I
wrote this story
during our voyage to
the Americas. We are
on a ship with a
cargo of many
enslaved Africans. I
began to get to know
some of them. One in
particular was a
young man named
Kyauta. He's near my

age and taught me so much. I've been punished countless times for talking to the slaves. He explained his route to freedom to me and how his father was brutally murdered in front of him. I simply cried. I had no way to even try to imagine his pain. I figured if I couldn't understand it, then I'm sure none of my people could either. So, I decided to write this fictional story about him and his people in order to help level the empathy. The last words Kyauta told me were, "I am free. I can now be with my father." Kyauta, with my assistance decided to jump ship. The pain of losing him was unbearable. I saw

him as a brother. It
was like looking in
the mirror. It was like
looking through a
telescope filled with
mirrors. My path
could have easily
been his. This was my
first look Inside the
Kaleidoscope. I saw
many ways my life
could have been....
Alexander of England

1512

Journey to the Americas

www.ingramcontent.com/pod-product-compliance
Lightning Source LLC
Chambersburg PA
CBHW051133250726
48655CB00007B/3036